A HISTORY OF METHODIST CHURCH ADADIA, NIGERIA

Map of Adadia in Uruan Local Government Area

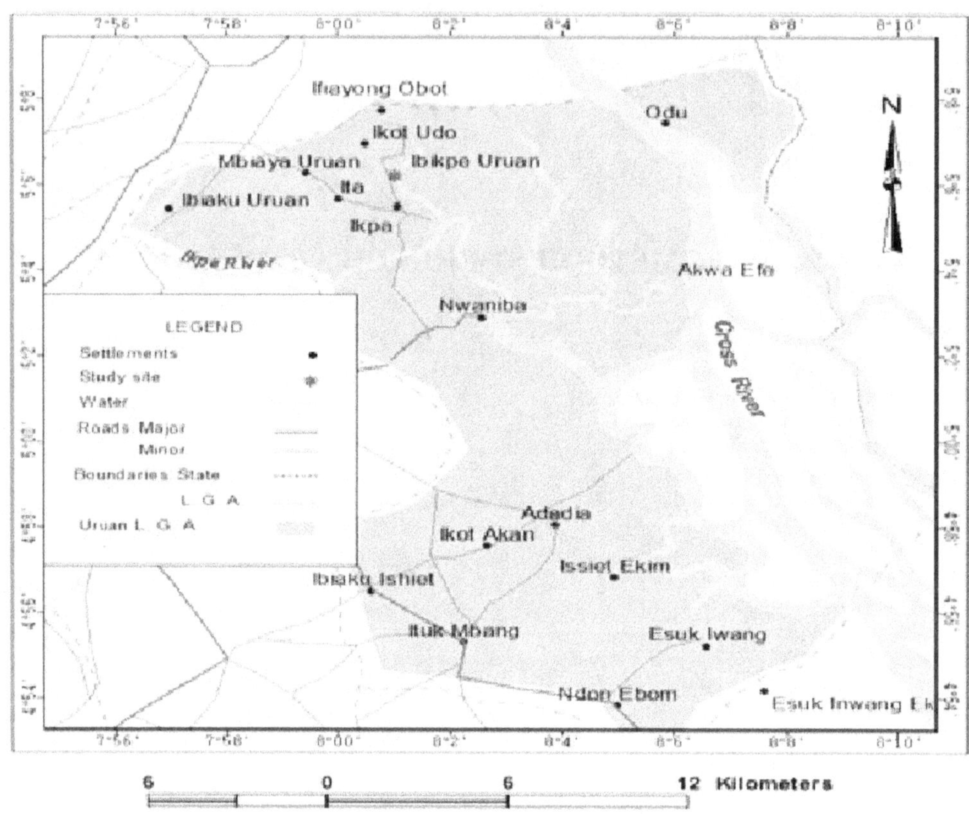

TABLE OF CONTENTS

CHAPTER ONE: INTRODUCTION

CHAPTER TWO: LAND AND THE PEOPLE OF ADADIA

CHAPTER THREE: HISTORY OF METHODIST CHURCH ADADIA

CHAPTER FOUR: IMPACT OF THE METHODIST CHURCH IN ADADIA CIRCUIT

CHAPTER FIVE: SUMMARY AND CONCLUSION

CHAPTER ONE: INTRODUCTION

Background

After the Niger Expedition, the Methodists were the first to exert Christian influence on Nigeria doing so with the arrival of William de Graft and Thomas Birch Freeman in Badagry on 23 September 1842. The story of the arrival of protestant missionaries in Nigeria came as a result of a strong plea that came from a returnee like James Ferguson and this plea was endorsed by the Governor of Badagry. The Primitive Methodist entered Eastern Nigeria with the arrival of Robber Farley in December 1893 from Fernando Po. Both merged in 1932 to form the Methodist Missionary Society. These slightly different strands of Methodism developed independently of each other into two separate districts of the British Church until they were finally united under the umbrella of the foundation as autonomous and autocephalous in September 1962. This effort generated aggressive mission work throughout Nigeria spreading the good news of Jesus Christ. This now gave birth to what is regarded as the citadel of Western civilization and commerce in Nigeria. The efforts of the Methodist Church in Nigeria go a long way in instituting holistic ministries and national Development.

Adadia town is located about sixteen kilometres East of Uyo, Akwa Ibom State Capital. It is the terminus of the land route from Uyo through Ifa Ikot Okpon and Mbak Etoi to Adadia. Another route into Adadia is Ibiaku Issiet or Ituk Mbang. The two villages are located on Uyo/Oron road. The last route is through the sea. This sea route is strategic to Adadia. The Creek meanders into the Calabar River and the Atlantic Ocean. In those days, when Southern Cameroon was part of Nigeria both Adadia and Cameroon traded unhindered until Southern Cameroon which is English speaking opted out of Nigeria to join the Cameroons who are French-speaking. The sea route explains why Adadia people are fishermen by nature and also explains why the event of the last century was possible. The town is in the tropics having its fair share of rainfall and sunshine. The people engage in fishing, farming and trading. Bolaji Ogundele noted, "The riverine people primarily engage in fishing and trading. Other vocations like handicrafts and farming are peripheral. Therefore, this study seeks to examine the history of Methodist Church Adadia, 1907-2010.

The Methodist Church Adadia has been at the forefront of spiritual and social transformation, by spreading spiritual holiness and investing in medical-health services and the socio-economic welfare of the people. The church has established various institutions and carter of the people in the Adadia community. These centres reach out to the rejected and less privileged members of society. They also ensure the reintegration of those previously treated as an outcast and subjected to various societal waves of abuse. In the area of health, Methodist Church Adadia has been known to be providing medical assistance to those with health issues in the community. In addition to all other services, Methodist Church Adadia has from the beginning placed a very strong emphasis on the need for education. Throughout the Adadia community, the church has established schools, from kindergarten through primary to senior secondary school which have produced men and women who have contributed and are still contributing very significantly to all spheres of human endeavour. This study seeks to examine the history of Methodist Church Adadia in Uruan Local Government Area, 1907-2010.

CHAPTER TWO: LAND AND THE PEOPLE OF ADADIA

Origin and Settlement

Uruan is located in the south of Nigeria and is a Local Government Area of the Akwa Ibom State. Uruan Local Government Area was created in 1988 from the Uyo Local Government Area. It covers an approximate land mass of 449 km2. Its population, according to the 2016 Census is 164,000. The Capital City of Uruan Local Government is Idu. The area lies in the rainforest belt with extensive arable land and the region abounds with wildlife, raffia palm and timber. The rich coastal plains support the cultivation of crops such as cassava and maize. Uruan people speak the Uruan language. Uruan people have maintained a good relationship with their neighbours. Their seven-clan structure is also maintained. This is the structure depicted during the coronation and burial of the Edidem Atakpor, the Nsomm of Uruan, by the presence of seven traditional bow-men, seven spear-men, seven sword-men, and seven royal staff-men each of which represents Essien Uruan.

The principal deity of the Uruan people is Atakpor, which was brought from the Southern Cameroons and is believed to be a Great Mother deity that associates with water. The Atakpor was regarded as a female deity and as an intermediary through which the Uruan people could communicate with Abasi (God). Today Uruan people believe that this Great Mother deity lives in that body of water now known as Akwa Akpa Uruan (The Mighty Sea of Uruan).

Other aspects of Uruan heritage include Ekpe, Ekong (War), Nka (Age-grade), Ebre, Fattening Home (Nkugho), and so on. Uruan people developed the idea of Ekpe society, used for maintaining law and order, and for entertainment. There are various grades of Ekpe, such as Nyamkpe, Nkanda, Mbökkö and Ibom. The Ekpe members of higher grades are known for their display of Nsibidi, secret writing or signs used for communication among the members. The Ekong is a traditional warrior society used for encouraging chivalry or bravery among men in Uruan. It was developed as an instrument for checking social ills and fostering security and unity among the people. The Ebre was a traditional society used by women for social and political control, and for the promotion of women's rights. Nka (Age-grades) in Uruan were used for the effective performance of different aspects of community work, mutual help and for the discipline of their members.

Uruan people developed the Uruan language which they derived from the proto-language. It is a variant of the Ibibio language. Uruan language is what has for historical reasons been referred to as the Efik language, and Uruan and Efik are all Iboku people. According to Uruan historians, like Dominus Essien of the University of Uyo and Edet Akpan Udo of *Who Are the Ibibios*, Uruan people are believed to have migrated in different waves from East-Central and Southern Africa to Uruan Akpe in the area now called Idomi in the Rio del Rey near the Southwest Region of Cameroon and Cross River State border where they settled for centuries. Due to the first Batanga war which caused economic and social disorder in the region, Uruan people migrated to an area in the Cross River Basin called Akani Obio Uruan in about the 8th century A.D. The river near the settlement was named Akwa Akpa Uruan meaning (Mighty River of Uruan).

It is believed that in the 13th century, hundreds of Uruan people, another Iboku group who also migrated through a different route joined their kindred at Akani Obio Uruan and Akpa Mfri Ukim. Due to geographical and ecological problems, such as frequent floods, Uruan people migrated again further to the mainland and occupied an area now known as Uruan Local Government Area in Akwa Ibom State. Due to social conflicts between some clans within Uruan, the

Akpe Iboku people of Uruan, now the Eburutu tribe, later nicknamed "Efik" migrated from Uruan Country (Essien Uruan Itiaba) to such places as Creek Town (Uruan Esit Edik), Duke Town (Uruan Ibuot Utan) and Henshaw Town (Nsidung). Until today, some Efik families still treasure their connections with some Uruan villages, such as Esuk Odu, Issiet Ekim, Mbiaya, Ibiaku Uruan, Adadia, Ndon Ebom, and Ekpene Ibia, most of which still speak Efik language.[5]

Clans

Of the original twelve traditional clans, only seven largely unrecognized clans remain today. Others are believed to have settled among the Ibibios such as Ekpene Ukim village in Nsit Ubium and Ikpa village in Eket. To date, these villages still maintain a strong bond with their Uruan kindreds.

The remaining seven clans are Akwa Uruan, comprising Nturukpum, Esuk Odu, Ibuno Issiet, Issiet Inua Akpa, Use Uruan, Issiet Ekim, Ekim-Enen, Afaha Ikot, Ikot Nkanga, Ama Odung, Ikot Owot, Esuk Issiet and Obio Nkan; Etongko Mkpe Uruan, comprising Ifiayong Obot, Obio Obot Osong, Osong, Akpa Utong, Ibikpe, Ikot Udo, and Mbiaya; Mutaka Uruan, comprising Ekpene Ibia, Ikot

Edung, Ibiaku Issiet, Obio Ndobo, Ikot Akpa Ekang, Ikot Akan and Adadia; Ekondo Uruan, comprising Ibiaku Ikot Ese, Ndon Uruan, Ituk Mbang, Ekpene Ukim, Ndon Ebom, Esuk Inyang, Nung Ikono Ufok, and Nung Ikono Obio; Mosongko Uruan, comprising Akpa Mfri Ukim, Esuk Anakpa, Ufak Obio Uruan, Akani Obio Uruan, Obio Akwa Akpa Uruan, Esuk Idu, Ikot Etuong, Ifiayong Esuk, Nwaniba, Mbiakong, Ifiayong Usuk, Eman Ikot Udo and Idu; Ibonda Uruan, comprising Edik Ikpa, Eman Ukpa, Anakpa, Nna Enin, Ikot Inyang Esuk, Nung Oku and Ikot Oto Inyie; Akpe Iboku Uruan, comprising Ibiaku, Eman, Utit, Ita, Ikpa, Ikot Oku and Esuk Ikpa. (Idu Uruan).

Origin of Adadia

Adadia town is located about sixteen kilometres East of Uyo, Akwa Ibom State Capital. It is the terminus of the land route from Uyo through Ifa Ikot Okpon and Mbak Etoi to Adadia. Another route into Adadia is Ibiaku Issiet or Ituk Mbang. The two villages are located on Uyo/Oron Road. The last route is through the sea. This sea route is strategic to Adadia. The Creek meanders into the Calabar River and the Atlantic Ocean. In those days, when Southern Cameroon was part of Nigeria both Adadia and Cameroon traded unhindered until Southern

Cameroon which is English-speaking opted out of Nigeria to join the Cameroon who are French-speaking.

The sea route explains why Adadia people are fishermen by nature and explains why the event of the last century was possible. The town is in the tropics having its fair share of rainfall and sunshine. The people engage in fishing, farming, and trading. Bolaji Ogundele noted, "The riverine people primarily engage in fishing and trading. Other vocations like handicrafts and farming are peripheral.

In core riverine communities, women and children often leave the main communities to go to the fishing settlements where they stay for days fishing and shrimping just to keep the family together. They are the most difficult people to access, and they lack basic amenities and motorable roads. Should any trip take one to a typical riverine community, what will hit the person on the face are structures parted into two segments by one road which terminates at a waterfront. In these places, the main road is the only visible road. One can access other parts of the road through footpaths which may pass through a swamp. Adadia enjoy this riverine life. Although Adadia people live on top of crude oil, lack of technology deprived them of the knowledge of this asset until 1957 when the first oil exploration by the Shell Company took place in the town. Duke, writing in his book *Adadia Circuit, Today and Yesterday* notes that Adadia is endowed with low soft hills slopping from West to East and disappearing in the Creeks that lead to the Cross River and finally into the Atlantic Ocean. Buried in the soft green hills are tons of gravel which the natives excavated during the building of the Pritchard Memorial Methodist Church in 1958. Essien reports that "there is silver nitrate in Adadia. It is also reported that there is Gas and Salt in Adadia". Apart from coastal contacts, Adadia at the time was secluded from Uyo where main activities took place. Their main means of transportation was by canoe. Bicycles were owned by the rich and going to Uyo Was done by trekking, a very energy-sapping exercise, indeed.

As expected, the coastal trade flooded the Adadia market with fish, crayfish, periwinkle, crab, and alcoholic drinks of all sorts, among other things. The Ogoja people brought yams and earthen pots through the Cross River. The means of trade was by barter and later using cowries, wire rods and manilla. Adadia Creek was well disposed to trading. As opposed to the waterway to Esuk-Odu and Ifiayong whose sand bank impeded entry during the ebb tide, the waterway to Adadia is deep and wide so that traders could still enter during the ebb tide. Adadia beach is also near the sea. Issiet Ekim has another deep-water way but is narrow and winding. The beach at Adadia has a continental shelf and which makes the approach to land easy and natural. With this natural setting, Adadia in terms of geography was destined to play host to the coming of the Europeans.

Culturally, Adadia was forced by the circumstances of her location to practice the worship of the riverine people. Like their Uruan brothers, they adopted the worship of Atakpo as their religion. Atakpo was believed to be a woman and the custodian of the soul of all Uruan people, who will not allow her children who earn their living from the sea to drown, even if they were ship-wrecked. Atakpo is attributed with the power to cause the people to float until rescue came. Smaller or lesser gods to Atakpo were also worshipped, such as Anwa Offiong, Iso Itiat, Iso Ekpenyong, mermaids, and many others. The worship of these gods/ goddesses implied the offer of sacrifices such as sheep, goats, eggs, hens, and assorted drinks. There were places of idol worship superintended by the Oku Ndem (Chief priest) whose duty was to intercede between the people and the gods. In cases of the late arrival of rains, barrenness in/ among women and all other natural phenomena, the Oku Ndem was consulted, and nobody dared disobey his prescription of various sacrifices for good harvest, peace in the land and fruitfulness among women.

Noah notes of the Ibibio people, "the office of the family head was often combined with that of the Chief priest of the family; and performed sacrifices at the shrines of the ancestors". The duty of the village head included sacrificing the shrines for the well-being of the village. Mothers of twins and their children were considered a curse on society and only their death or ex-communication could avert calamity for the people. This was followed by lavish sacrifices to appease the gods. Men married many wives as polygamy was not just a plurality of wives but a symbol of a communal way of life in family compounds. In place of Christmas celebration, they celebrated the New Year with much fanfare and sacrificed to the gods to bless them in the coming New Year. Nobody ate new yams until sacrifices were made to the gods of harvest. Sacrifices were performed every two years or leap year to ensure that calamities were averted, *etuak ndok, ewa nwomo*. As for recreation and social life, traditional plays of Ekpe, Ekpo, Obon, Ukwa, Epri Akata, Ebre, and Ekombi were observed.

Ekpe cultural plays were predominantly the administrative machinery of the people, for, as Udoema notes, "although there are many secret societies in Ibibio land, the next important one for the enforcement of judicial function was Ekpe." Adadia left Uruan Akpe (Efut Usuk) in Southern Cameroon and after their third wave of migration settled at their present abode called, addressed, and known as Itu Obio Amin to date. They indulged in the cultural plays that they carried along during their movement. Soon they discovered that the Ekpe they brought was of a lower rank than the ones played in Creek Town. So during the reign of Ekanem Ekpouta, he went into agreement with seven other villages of Uruan which were Issiet Ekim, Use Uruan, Esuk Odu, Afaha Ikot, Ekim Enen, Eman Ukpa and Anakpa to go and buy the complete order of Ekpe. The eight villages of Uruan (Essien Uruan Itiaita) were led by Chief Ekpo Eyo of Creek Town and they bought the complete order of Ekpe Nicanda, Okpoho and Oku Akama from the village head of Creek Town by the name, Chief Eyo Ema. They were given the pillar of the authority of Ekpe (Itiat Ekpe). Adadia erected theirs at the shrine at Adadia thus acquiring the highest full order of Ekpe to use in the administration of their village and for recreation.

To emphasize how influential Ekpe society and its authority were, they used it to force the people both men and women, irrespective of their religious faith, to go to the soft hills to excavate gravel for the construction of the church in 1958, when the foundation of the Methodist Church, Adadia was laid. This same authority was used to cause the people to fetch gravel for the building of both the Samuel Spiritual Church and the Apostolic Church to mention but a few. It should also be noted that Ekpe has a unifying influence. Ajayi noted, "there were internal rivalries between the various houses in each town. But despite these divisions, the Efik developed in the Egbo or more correctly Ekpe society, an organization covering the whole of Calabar and superseding the sectional interest." This unifying force of Ekpe was not only notified of the Efik but was also true of the Uruan neighbours of which Adadia is a part. Although Adadia people arrived at their abode in three different canoes headed by Emuk, Oto and Udo, Ekpe's cultural play was to knit them into one village. Only initiated members had the right to recreate when was played. Wives of members and their female children were free to go out when Ekpe was played. Ekpe also had economic functions. Besides members having free food and wine from an initiate's house during the period of his initiation into Ekpe society, some portions of farmlands were set aside from where only Ekpe members could cultivate or harvest oil palm fruits. The judicial function of Ekpe was honoured when people quarrelled over something. Ekpe injunction was invoked so that nobody could trespass until the dispute was settled and the rightful owner was known. If someone stole or was suspected to have caused the death of another person, he had to swear by the Ekpe oath, *ata etap ekpe*. It is generally believed that the guilty one would die and so people desisted from telling lies. Ekpe caused people to abjure in all matters be it stealing, witchcraft, farm dispute, and so on.

Ekpe has the authority to excommunicate a non-conforming citizen until he conforms. During the period of ex-communication, nobody greeted him or answered his greetings. He could not mix freely in society or enjoy the privileges of a citizen, *ewuk ofuro*. These privileges would be restored once he obeys the town's laws. Although Adadia had an ekpo masquerade, ekpe overshadowed its importance. For leisure and entertainment, Ekpri Akata was played. The function of Ekpri Akata was to expose social vices such as adultery, stealing and fornication. Ebre, the female counterpart of Ekpe, was played mainly by women. It acted as the barometer of social conscience and moral uprightness.

Udo states that "Ebre was a club. All married women in a village were expected to join it. The club had social and judicial functions. Its social functions included among others the staging of plays whenever a new member joined the club, and when a member dies. The judicial function of the club was very clear. Their law was that no member however poor must commit theft. Any erring member was expelled and punished thereby reducing the incidence of stealing in the society".[22] They were made to dance naked in the market square.

Another leisure play was Obon used mainly for burying people, especially those who died in mysterious circumstances. Ayandele aptly captures the picture of the society before the advent of Christianity. "The society they had left behind was prescriptive - the members being expected to conform to laws, norms and habitudes immemorially in existence."[23] This was the pattern of life prevalent in Uruan and -beyond at the time. Adadia being a part of Uruan was not immune to this prescriptive society, perpetually in conformity with the laws of the land.

It has already been mentioned, that Adadia people and their neighbours treated mothers of twins as those who brought curses on the land and so were to drink from separate sources of water not used by the entire town. In the same vein, those who died of smallpox were not buried in a coffin but were left in a thick forest, in a standing position leaning against a tree to rot away. It was generally believed that the ghost of smallpox victims roamed around and if the dead were buried near the town, it would provoke their spirits to cause many more people to catch the disease. Infants were laid on plantain leaves while their mothers lay near the fire until the children were able to sit. In short, the pre-Christianity status of the Adadia people was both pathetically superstitious and fanatically religious. Be that as it may, the traditional life was rewarding and enjoyable as feasting and eating were involved. A man who wanted to eat his wife's fowl could refuse her food for a few days and the wife would be forced to buy a fowl and cook for him as punishment for keeping the husband hungry.

A young boy had to remain an apprentice to his father studying the art of fishing until he was old enough to be given his own canoe and fishing nets by his father. The Gift of a room in the father's compound was indicative of the fact that he was mature for marriage to raise his own family. A small girl also had to undergo an apprenticeship with her mother before being confined and fattened to prepare her for marriage. She was circumcised before confinement. This was the society satisfying the local needs of the people until trade which brought them in contact with their neighbours in Calabar forced on them the diluted mode of living and brought a kind of cultural revolution in Adadia in 1899.

History and Culture

The first soil on which Adadia (Itu Obio Amin) lived was Uruan Ekpe in Efut in Southern Cameroon. Obong Ekene Iyitö led them and sailed up the Cross River, settled in the upland forest where Obio Oko (Creek Town) lives until this day.[26] The five villages that later joined them were: Adiabo, Obutöñ, Atakpa, Nsiduñ, and Ekpe Oku Atai (otherwise known as Mbarakom).

When Obong Ekene Iyitö died, a silk cotton tree was planted to mark his grave. His son, Iyitö Ekene Iyitö, was named after his grandfather led the next phase of migration and founded Esuk Mbat, which is Esuk Ekpok Ekpa, which is Okoyong Inua Akpa. He named it "Itu Iyitö Ekene." Obong Iyitö Ekene's team met Efot Abua living in one part of the land leading to Idim Ete Niñ. When Obong Iyitö Ekene died, his son, Amin Iyitö Ekene, renamed the place "Itu Obio Amin" meaning "Obio Ndito Iyitö Ekene," village of the descendants of Iyitö Ekene.

The Name, *Adadia*

When Obong Amin Iyitö Ekene died, ten young warriors went head hunting for the burial rites as was the custom then. They sailed and landed at Okobo. The Okobo people captured them and allocated them as slaves to their Chiefs. On some mornings when out from their masters' homes, they would discuss and plan their escape. One eventful evening, the captives decided to escape, they brought out some bottles of intoxicating drink, which they called *onwong otop eköt* and presented them to their masters who happily accepted and drank them. Being highly intoxicated they fell asleep. At night, they killed their masters and escaped. The Okobo people mourned and exclaimed "Idia Idia owo nyin." Giving rise to the name Adadia. The quarrel between Okon Otu Ukpong, an Okoyong son and Mbesembe Otu, led to war and caused Adadia to leave Okoyong for their present abode.[28] Among those who first left Okoyong for what is now known as Adadia were: Udo Obon, Andañ, Ema, Uma Eyie, Udo Obon, Mbo Nta, and Ekanem Akpakan. All these left with their families and on arriving at the new-found land, they settled at different locations.

Udo Obon: On arrival, founded a market, planted an African oil bean tree (Ukana), buried the ball of a bell, *efik nkanika*, plus an earthen cup, *tombit mbat*, and the market was called "Urua Udo Obong." **Andañ:** He arrived and founded his market and planted *udara* tree, and African star apple) and the market was called "Urua Ikot Essien Andan." **Umana Eyie:** He also arrived and founded his market, and planted a silk cotton tree. The market was called "Urua Umana Eyie." It was popularly called "Urua Enwaig Iban." **Mbo Nta:** Arrived a founded his market called "Okop Edi Iköñ Ekpañ." **Ekanem Akpakan:** On arrival found him and gave him two names "Ikot Oto" and "Ikot Akpakan." Akpabio Eda later arrived with Iba Etok. Andan was happy because they were the people who stood by them during the war. Iban also arrived and planted *ewan* tree in his area and called "Ewan Iban." Others who also arrived were Ubom Obio Ema, Oto Akpabio, Ikpoto Iyonko and Onion Ndem.

The three main family units of Adadia which migrated to the new land of Adadia were, Ekpuk Obong Ema from Nung Emuk landed in Akwa Esuk, Adadia otherwise called Esuk Atai; Ekpuk Obong Ubom Obio Ema from Ikot Udo landed and established a beach known as Esuk Ikot Ikpata; Ekpuk Obong Oto Akpabio Eda from Ikot Oto landed at Esuk Atai. Present-day Adadia has come to have gazette villages within it, which are: Esuk Akpan Ambo (Odoro Enen, Ikot Udo), Afaha Ikot, and Issiet Adadia (Issiet Inua Akpa).

Headship of Adadia

The Headship of Adadia otherwise known as "Obong Adadia" follows a rotational system within the three main outstanding family units namely: Nung Emuk, Ikot Udo and Ikot Ottor in its governance. When headship returns to a family unit, members of the family meet in their general house meeting and select a candidate of their choice and present to the Council of Village Heads for further screening and acceptance or no acceptance of the candidate to the council. When approval of a candidate is given by the Council of Chiefs, which normally should be a written note of information to the family Unit concerned, the unit shows appreciation and the candidate is introduced to them. Never at any point in the history of Adadia, had a non-indigene been appointed as "Obong Adadia" even though many live in the many family units.[30]

Names of "Obong Adadia", year, family unit

Obong Obioema (founder Main Beach), Ikot Udo
Obong Oŋwungedi Essien, Ikot Ottor

Obong Akadi, Nung Emuk

Obong Ubom Obioema (The Goddess High Priest), Ikot Udo

Obong Akpakan (Founder of Ekim Enen), Ikot Ottor

Obong Ekanim Ekpo Uta, 1887–1910,

Obong Akpan Effiong Inyang, 1910–1913, Nung Emuk

Obong Umo Okor, 1913–1921, Nung Udatim, Ikot Ottor

Obong Okor Udo, 1922–1924, Ata Essien, Ikot Ottor

Obong Eduok Akpanteng, 1924–1930, Ikot Ekpot, Nung Emuk

Obong Akpan Udo, Nov. 1930–47, Odoro Enen, Ikot Udo

Obong Efiong Etim Akpan Ndon, 1948–1951, Ikot Akpan, Ikot Ottor

Obong Efiong Inyang Udo, 1952–1976, Ikot Enang, Nung Emuk

Obong Ekpenyong Etim Offiong, 1977–1988, Nung Eda, Ikot Udo

Obong Bassey Asukwo Essien, 1989–2001, Ata Essien, Ikot Ottor

Obong Etim Udo Ekaeba, 2002 - date, Ikot Abia Ntem, Nung Emuk

Institution of Nsomship

The founding fathers developed the chieftaincy institution in their original home in Southwestern Cameroun and brought it with them to Uruan, where they developed the Edidem Atakpor throne. The Nsomm of Uruan is the head of the institution. The Edidem or Nsomm is the paramount traditional ruler of all the seven Uruan clans. In Uruan, chieftaincy was and is a sacred institution. The holder of Nsomm's title must be a free-born and a bona fide son of Uruan whose ancestry must be traced back to the Royal Stock of Uruan Inyang Atakpor. The Nsomm must acknowledge Atakpor as the Supreme Deity of Uruan land and its people and therefore becomes his chief custodian. The title of the earlier custodians was not Nsomm, but nonetheless, their role was perhaps more important than any other single individual in Uruan. Their primary function was to go from one Atakpor shrine to another performing sacrifice to the great deity, Atakpor. It is believed that these men had no home to call theirs since they had to be on the move most of the time. They were housed and fed by the people of the community in which they happened to find themselves. These men were totally committed to the work of Atakpor.

Selection of Nsomm

It became a laid down law that for one to be selected a paramount ruler of Uruan or Nsomm of Uruan, one must first be a village head. A qualified village head is selected by the Uruan Council of Chiefs when its members formally meet as kingmakers. The selection of Nsomm is made based on merit, intelligence, ability, influence, and integrity. Of late, the educational background has been added as one of the requirements. Thus, a stranger, an illegitimate, a thief or a wicked person is not allowed to ascend the royal throne of the Nsomm of Uruan. Nsomm's office is not a dynasty, therefore not inherited; but the title and office are founded on a tradition of unbroken succession.

The Nsomm of Uruan has an advisory council and he selects members from Uruan village heads. As the custodian of Uruan customs and traditions, the Nsomm has a prerogative of appointing accredited sons and daughters of Uruan to the Nsomm Advisory Council. Village heads who are members of the council are first-class chiefs in Uruan clan. Honorary chiefs are second-class chiefs; other members of the council are the Etubom. Both the second-class chiefs and Etubom can attend the council as observers but cannot cast any vote in the council.

CHAPTER THREE: HISTORY OF METHODIST CHURCH ADADIA

A Brief Introduction to Methodist Church

Christianity was established in Nigeria with the arrival in 1842 of a Wesleyan Methodist Church missionary. He had come in response to the request for missionaries by the ex-slaves who returned to Nigeria from Sierra Leone. From the mission stations established in Badagry and Abeokuta, the Methodist church spread to various parts of the country west of the River Niger and part of the north. In 1893 missionaries of the Primitive Methodist Church arrived from Fernando Po, an island off the southern coast of Nigeria. From there the Methodist Church spread to other parts of the country, east of the River Niger and also to parts of the North. The church west of the River Niger and part of the north was known as the Western Nigeria District and east of the Niger and another part of the north as the Eastern Nigeria District. Both existed independently of each other until 1962 when they constituted the Conference of Methodist Church Nigeria. The conference is composed of seven districts. The church has continued to spread into new areas and has established a department for outreach/evangelism and appointed a director of evangelism. An episcopal system adopted in 1976 was not fully accepted by all sections of the church until the two sides came together and resolved to end the disagreement. A new constitution was ratified in 1990. The system is still episcopal but the points which caused discontent were amended to be acceptable to both sides.

The Methodist Church Nigeria is headed by the prelate, who presides over the conference, the overall governing body of the church. This conference meets every two years to deliberate and take decisions on all issues affecting the life of the church. The conference area is divided into eight archdioceses. Each archdiocese is composed of not less than four dioceses over which an archbishop presides at the archdiocesan council meetings. There are 44 dioceses, each made up of several circuits and headed by a bishop who presides over the annual synod. The constitution of the church provides for lay participation in the leadership of the church from the local church through to the conference level.

The Beginning of the Methodist Church in Nigeria

Methodist Church Nigeria started 170 years ago through the missionary activities of Rev. Thomas Birch Freeman. On September 24, 1842, Birch Freeman accompanied by two devoted African workers, Mr and Mrs Williams

De-Graft Johnson, arrived in Badagry from Gold Coast present-day Ghana. According to history, Methodism is the first Christian Mission in Nigeria. The work in Western Nigeria was pioneered by the Wesleyan Methodist Mission while the Primitive Methodist Mission pioneered missionary activities in Eastern Nigeria in December 1893. Among the pioneers in the Eastern Region were Rev. C. Fairley and Rev. Ben Showell. The two missions worked in their respective regions until 1932 when they were amalgamated and formed the present-day Methodist Church Nigeria. Although at this point, they operated as two Districts of Methodism – the Western and the Eastern District under the direction of the Methodist Church Britain. On September 28, 1962, Methodist Church Nigeria became autonomous from the British Methodist Conference with its corporate headquarters at Wesley House, 21/22 Marina, Lagos State.

Rev. Dr J. O. E. Soremekun became the first elected president followed by Rev. N. O. Salako. He died before the end of his tenure. Rev. N. O. Salako's tenure coincided with the Civil War period. Rev. Prof. Bolaji Idowu took over from Rev. N. O. Salako on October 4, 1972. The tenure of Rev. Prof. Bolaji Idowu witnessed the flowering of the Methodist Church in Nigeria. Rev. Prof. Bolaji Idowu moved the Church from its Foundation Constitution to the adoption of Episcopacy. In 1976, the church adopted a new constitution which gave birth to the present-day Episcopal system of the Church. The leader of the Church in the 1976 constitution became known as Patriarch and addressed as His Pre-Eminence.

Shortly after the adoption of Episcopacy, some sections of the Church became dissatisfied with the new constitution. This led to a schism which lasted about 14 years. During this period, Patriarch Bolaji Idowu retired and His Pre-Eminence, Sunday C. Mbang was elected as Patriarch in 1984. His Pre-Eminence Mbang worked assiduously to resolve the crisis. Between late 1989 and 1990, His Eminence, Mbang convened a series of meetings and Conferences of Methodist people to fashion a solution to the crisis. To the glory of God, the crisis came to an end in 1990 when a new Constitution was ratified on 24 May 1990, during a Unification Service at Hoare's Memorial Methodist Cathedral, Yaba.

In the 1990 Constitution, the Church adopted the title Prelate for her leader. Since the unification of the Church, the Methodist Church has remained one of the most formidable religious organizations in the country. In 2006, His Eminence Sunday C. Mbang handed over the mantle of leadership of the Church to the present Prelate, His Eminence Dr Sunday Ola Makinde. The assumption of

His Eminence Dr Sunday Ola, Makinde into office coincided with the adoption of a new constitution in 2006. From a humble beginning, Methodist Church in Nigeria has spread across the length and breadth of this country. At the moment the Church has 80 Dioceses and 17 Archdioceses. Methodist Church is known for its reputation in establishing Colleges, Teachers' Training Institutions, Social Welfare and Rehabilitation Centers, and Community Mental Health programs among many other social and human service projects and programs. Methodist Church Nigeria recently established Wesley University of Science and Technology, Ondo (WUSTO), Ondo State, Nigeria. The first set of students of the University graduated in 2012. Famous institutions include The Leprosy Centre, Uzuakoli, and Amaudo Centre for Mentally Ill Destitute. Under the Methodist Church Nigeria Constitution, all properties are vested in the Registered Trustees of the Church. Presently, the Church is led by the Prelate, the Secretary of Conference who also by his office is the Secretary of the Board of Registered Trustees, Bishops' Council and Conference Connexional Council.

The Arrival of the Methodist Missionaries in Nigeria around 1840

The Yoruba settlers in Freetown, Sierra / Leone had appealed to the Queen of England to permit them to establish a Colony in Badagry. They also demanded that soldiers, traders, and missionaries be sent to them at Badagry to help them wage war against slavery, especially the Ado people, and to preach the Gospel of Christ.[8] In 1841, these people wrote letters to missionaries who were stationed in Sierra Leone to come and preach the gospel of Christ in Badagry. When their letters were read to the Christians in Sierra Leone, some people liked the idea and appealed to missionaries to assist the Christians in Badagry.

On 24 September 1842, the Reverend Thomas Birch Freeman and William de Graft arrived at Badagry. Reverend Freeman preached the gospel to the people who lived in Badagry. He made many converts in the town. The Clergy built a mission house at Badagry. He organized prayer meetings for the Christians. Freeman paid a visit to Abeokuta to open a mission station in Egbaland. When he got to Abeokuta, he met Henry Townsend an Anglican Catechist and two Egba-freed slaves from Sierra Leone spreading the gospel there. When he returned from Abeokuta to Badagry, he left for his home country. Freeman left De Graft behind at Badagry to care for the adherents of the Methodist faith both in Badagry and

Abeokuta respectively. However, he used to pay visits to De Graft once in a blue moon. The Methodist mission later transferred De Graft and posted Samuel Annear to replace him at Badagry. The mission station at Abeokuta was shut down due to the Dahomey wars for a period by the Methodist Mission. However, when the war ended, a teacher was sent there to reopen the Mission Station at Abeokuta. The Methodist outreaches spread from Badagry to Lagos. In addition to the above-named means used to spread Christianity in the Yoruba land, mention could be made of the freed slaves who went from Sierra Leone to settle at Abeokuta after gaining their freedom from the Dahomean armies.

In 1846, the Methodist and Anglican Missions were established in Lagos and Abeokuta. Besides, as soon as the Lagos slave market was shut down, the Methodist and Anglican Missionaries entered there, and they established Mission Stations and Schools in both towns. African ministers were stationed in the two towns to spread Christianity.[10] In the Schools that were established by the missionaries in Lagos and Abeokuta towns, instructions were largely oral since books were scarce. Prayers and Biblical texts were learnt through oral recitation. Christianity could not penetrate the Northern parts of Nigeria in the early period, because the then Governor-General of Nigeria, Sir Lord Lugard ruled that Christianity could only be allowed to enter the Hausa land through the agreement of the ruling Chiefs who were the Custodians of Islam religion.

The Baptist Mission

In 1850, the American Baptist Missionary, Thomas J. Bowen arrived Badagry. He established a mission station there. He built a Mission Station at Ijaye. In the same year, he moved from there to Abeokuta. There he met the Wesleyan and the Church Missionary Society Missionaries. While Bowen was in the town, he studied the Yoruba language to be able to communicate with the people without any interpreter. He later wrote Yoruba Grammar and Dictionary for the use of Yoruba people. Bowen proceeded from Abeokuta to Ibadan and Ogbomosho where he established Baptist Mission Stations in 1854.

At Ogbomosho, converts saw themselves as superior people over the traditionalists. For this reason, the traditionalists developed hatred against Christians in the town. Besides, they abandon the tradition of burying the dead in their family compounds. This act compounded their problems in the town. Christians then started burying their dead in the bush. This is because Christians considered the practice of burying the dead in residential houses unhygienic.[13] On the other hand, traditionalists viewed burying the dead in the bush as a separation from their ancestors. In traditional beliefs, the moment a person is dead, he has become an ancestor, to be reverenced and worshipped. The traditionalists hated the Christians the more for not allowing the buried Christians to join their ancestors. The traditionalists also kicked against the idea of the Christians burying the dead in the bush for only criminals were buried in the bush at Ogbomosho. In 1879, according to Ayandele, all Christians were expelled from Ogbomoso. Bowen built a Mission station at Ijaye.

In 1854, Harden also established a Mission Station in Lagos, Lagos State, Nigeria. From Lagos, the Baptist Mission also spread to Oyo, Shaki, and Igboho, all in Oyo State, and Ilorin, in Kwara State, Nigeria. The spread of the Baptist Mission to the Northern parts of Nigeria was done by some Nigerians who were working in Northern Nigeria. The Government posted them to the place after the Second World War. The Yoruba government workers in the North were located mostly in Jos. There they worshipped as adherents of the Baptist faith. However, in 1912, the Nigerian Baptist Convention was officially formed. It is now completely self-governing, self-propagating, and self-supporting. In 1920, a Minister of the faith paid a visit to them. There he officially established a Mission Station for the Baptist adherents. While he was returning from Jos, he stopped at

Kaduna and established a Mission Station for the Yorubas who lived in the town. He baptized eighteen people in River Kaduna. In 1913, Mr M A. Adeniran established the first Baptist Mission Station in Zaria. According to Crampton, the Nigerian Baptist Convention posted Reverend J.A. Adejumobi to Kaduna as its first Pastor to oversee the rest Mission Stations of the Baptist faith in Northern Nigeria in the year 1925.

Furthermore, when the American and some of the Nigerian Missionaries worked together in the Northern parts of the country they established a Secondary School at Jos, a Teacher Training College in Minna and a Seminary School in Kaduna. The Nigerian Baptist Convention operates nine theological training centres for pastors, the largest being the Nigerian Baptist Theological Seminary in Ogbomosho. The Nigerian Baptist Convention also operates several hospitals and medical institutions across the country. The Baptist Hospital in Ogbomosho remains one of the leading hospitals in Nigeria. Besides, it is used as a University teaching hospital by the Ladoke Akintola University jointly owned by Oyo and Osun states. In 1969, a separate Conference for Ilorin and Ka a faithful was established and it was named Kwara Baptist Conference. The Church has planted about 100 Mission Stations in the Area. Besides, a group of Longuda who broke away from the Lutheran faith joined the Baptist faith in Northern Nigeria.

In 1972, Etubi who was a missionary in the Qua Ibo Church at Idah broke away and joined the Baptist. In 1974, a second Baptist church was established at Idah it is named Emmanuel Baptist Church, Idah. The Baptist Mission has the Northern Conference Convention, which has its Headquarters at Beulah. It comprises Adamawa and Sardauna Provinces. The Mission Stations are in the following towns, Zaria, Kano, Katsina and Sokoto. The Nigerian Baptist Convention has founded and operated several primary Schools and Secondary Schools across the nation. The Mission has established a University at Iwo in 2002. It is named Bowen University in honour of Reverend Thomas Jefferson Bowen, the first American Baptist Missionary from the Southern Baptist Convention. The named institutions above are established to convert pupils, Secondary school students and post-secondary school students into the Baptist faith in Nigeria to date.

In 1969, a separate Conference for Ilorin and Kaba faithful was established, and it was named Kwara Baptist Conference. The Church has planted about 100 Mission Stations in the Area. Besides, a group of Longuda who broke away from the Lutheran faith joined the Baptist faith in Northern Nigeria. In 1972, Etubi, who was a Missionary in the Qua Ibo Church at Idah, broke away and joined the Baptist. In 1974, a second Baptist Church was established at Idah, it was named Emmanuel Church, Idah. The Baptist Mission has the Northern Conference Convention, which has its Headquarters at Beulah. The Mission Stations were in the following towns: Zaria, Kano, Katsina and Sokoto. The Nigerian Baptist Convention has founded and operated several Primary Schools and Secondary Schools across the nation. The Mission established a University at Iwo in 2002. It is named Bowen University in honour of Reverend Thomas Jefferson Bowen, the first American Baptist Missionary from the Southern Baptist Convension.

The Advent of the Church of Scotland Mission in Adadia

Whatever informed the people of Adadia to desert or at best to dilute their traditional form of worship of many years in preference to the Christian religion, our generation may not fully know. What is certain is that the study of Adadia may have to take us over many decades. Even at that, the number of years we shall have to go back to reach a beginning, which was not a beginning, is a matter of speculation which may produce widely different interpretations and answers.

From available records, the sixteenth village head of Adadia was Obong Udosen Akpan Ekanem. As the fifteen village heads before him starting from Chief Ekene Eyito; Eyito Ekene Eyito; Amin Eyito Ekene; Abasi Amin Eyito Ekene; Akpabio Amin Eyito; Antia Amin Eyito; Offiong Amin Eyito; Umo Amin Eyito; Mbuotidem Amin Eyito; Ekpo Amin Eyito; Idang Amin Eyito; Oko Udo Ndobo; Ubom Akpan Udosen; Akata Eda; and Akpan Udosen Uwang Eto, no dates are attached to their reign. Even Udosen Akpan Ekanem is recorded to have died in 1886.

No one could say when his reign began. The chief who stands out in Adadia as the person intervening in the affairs of Adadia between the past and the present was Ekanem Ekpo Uta (1887 - 1910). He gave Adadia visitors lands to live in, such as Okon Udo Akpa and Chief Etim Udo Akpa. It was agreed that the highest rank of Ekpe should be brought from Creek Town. He was a young man when the Church of Scotland Mission entered Calabar in 1846. Just as Chief Ekanem Ekpo Uta sent to buy the highest order of Ekpe for Adadia in like manner, he sent for the Church of Scotland Mission to be established in his village. Succeeding Chiefs helped in turning Adadia into Christ. They were Etim Efiong Ayaya (1911 - 1912); Umo Nko (1913 - 1921); Eduok Akpa Nteng (1922 -

1934); Akpan Udo Ibe (1935 - 1948); Efiong Etim Akpa Ndono (1949 - 1951); Efiong Inyang Udo Ntong (1952 - 1976); Ekpenyong Etim Ayaya (1977 - 1988); Bassey Asuquo Esien (1989 -2001); Okon Etim Udo Ekaeba (2004 till date). These chiefs were relevant in the century we are celebrating because without their support the church could not have been established especially in those difficult days in Adadia. The Presbyterian Mission entered Calabar in 1846.

Essien writes "Rev. Hope Waddel and his team were led by John Beecroft, Governor of Fernan do Po to Old Calabar in 1846. Later the Presbyterian planted missionary seed in Creek Town and in the surrounding villages." Ajayi, notes that on reaching Calabar in April 1846, Hope Waddel saw that, particularly in the Delta, trade, not agriculture, was the civilizing force, and that the Chiefs were not a "land-owning aristocracy" but middle-class traders. Aided by their coastal nature, Uruan people and Adadia in particular had maintained contact with the Efik traders. In his publication, "Calabar: A colonial casualty." Nwaka, observes, "It is recorded that sometime in the 17th century possibly a little earlier, the "Efiks... migrated southwards from Uruan and located themselves in the neighbourhood of Creek Town."' The migration of the Efiks from Uruan meant the extension of the area of influence of the Adadia people and Uruan in general.

Adadia people had been exchanging various items of trade with their Efik brothers. They intermarried with them, and so their lives were, therefore, not unaffected by the changes that occasioned the advent of Christianity in Calabar in 1846. Ajayi notes that Hope Waddel's arrival at Calabar met "King Eyo's son keep accounts, writing and copying into account book the memoranda of business which his father had made on slate... neatly entered and all in English. Adadia people naturally desired to "import" home this "magic" of the white man which enabled the son of King Eyo to speak in English and write his Village Head father's accounts of sales in English.[25] To the Adadia people, the Christian religion was the answer. For as Ajayi noted, the chiefs and traders wanted not just worthless finery, but tools and machinery, and they wanted also that their children should be taught European languages, how to keep account and so on". The only way to acquire this priceless knowledge was through religion.

It was this zeal for new ways of life that caused Obong Ekanem Ekpo Uta, the village head of Adadia in council in 1899, to send these six young sons of Adadia in the persons of Efiong Etim, Efiong Inyang Udo, Edet Eduok, John Udo Orok, Inyang Asuquo Adiaha Umo and Obot Akpan Nnana to Creek Town to bring the religion to Adadia. The young men got to Creek town and got baptized into the Church of Scotland Mission. Effiong Etim and John Udo Orok got their wives Nkoyo Essien Ikpa and Nyong Inyang Udo respectively to be baptized into the Church of Scotland Mission and blessed their marriages. One of them Edet Eduok lost his wristwatch during the search for Christianity. They returned to Adadia to form the nucleus of the Church of Scotland Mission. The house of Obong Ansa Akpan Akpe Ekpe was used for Assembly to hold divine services until they constructed a church building for Seventeen Pounds or Thirty-Four Naira and transferred the church there. The church cemetery testifies to this. Last burials there were in 1918 and 1919 respectively.[26]

The new wave of life brought about by the advent of the Church of Scotland Mission impacted positively on the people of Adadia. The few Adadia people who joined the church started to talk and write in English however imperfect it was, to impress on people that the new religion was good. As the contact between the Efiks of Creek Town and the people of Adadia deepened so also were the advantages of the new religion. The people of Adadia then invited the Mission to start work in Adadia in 1902. The church also started at Issiet Ekim, a few kilometres away in the same year. The teachers in Adadia were Essien Itam and Edet Abasi Ekpriowo of Creek Town.[27]

The Church appointed Rev. Wear as a visiting Minister while Mr Essien Itam and Edet Abasi Ekpriowo of Creek Town were the teachers. The enthusiasm with which the church was received started to wane as the method of imparting knowledge by the Church of Scotland teachers was not only draconic but merciless. People were forcefully removed from their houses to go to church. Sir Edet Nnsewo, captures graphically the action of the Church of Scotland Mission in his book, *Brief History of Methodist Church Ikot Akpa Etok* noted that "as a one-teacher school, Mr Hogan Bassey became the be all and end all of everything. He recruited only boys (men) of ten to twenty-five years of age. He told the people that all boys of 15 - 25 years were his pupils and must come to school. Within a month, he was able to raise enough lads to go on a raid for pupils in the surrounding villages. The school itself became regimental. The father of an offender was arrested and taken to Hogan Bassey's Court where he was found guilty of keeping a pupil at home and heavily fined." These dictatorial tendencies were unpleasant to the Ikot Akpa Etok people as well as it was regimental to the Adadia people.[28]

There was no work on Sundays among other things. The school they established practised corporal punishment. Faced with the draconic laws coupled with strict discipline and flogging, it was not sudden that the Church of Scotland Mission lacked volunteer youths in the church and school, so the salary of the church workers was outstanding and could not be paid. Adadia church celebrated its Golden Jubilee in 1957 and wrote in the souvenir publication that "the Church of Scotland Mission ran into problems with the people of Adadia congregation as they were unable to secure readily 12000 wire-rods which was a monthly salary of the teacher."[29]

The collapse of the Church of Scotland Mission was not unexpected. People could not bear the high punishment and taxation any longer. Some chiefs from Ikot Akpa Etok and beyond lodged a complaint with the Colonial Resident in Uyo. Mr Hogan Bassey alias Okon Abakpa of Akim Qua Town, Calabar was "apprehended, charged and imprisoned for six months." His imprisonment led to the loss of credibility in the church and school. The work of the mission was therefore terminated in 1906.[30]

Although there was no radical change in the people's way of life, as far as their superstitious tendency was concerned, they, still followed their traditional religion side by side with the new religion. Church members were still initiated into traditional practices. During the African end of the year, Ekpo play was celebrated. Eka Ekpo was sent to the beyond (Ekpat Eka Ekpo). There was no play of Ekpo for six months except when a member died. A woman whose husband died was subjected to a dehumanizing experience. Her head was shaved, and she was to stay without a bath until the funeral ceremonies were over. Women were not to eat plantain joined together. The plantain must be separated halfway, and separation completed behind her back as her hands still holding the partially separated plantain would complete the separation.[31]

This was to avert the woman from giving birth to Siamese twins. To keep off polio, a leaf, *Okono* was placed across the doorpost of a nursing mother so that if a mother who had a child attacked by polio enters the house the young baby will not be attacked by polio or convulsion. A person who did not collect enough items or complete the burial of his parents could not eat at a person's funeral or she would die. Women were prevented from entering certain streams for some weekdays or they would disappear or be attacked by python snakes. Superstitious as these beliefs were, they were held dear by the people including the church members.[32]

Libation was poured before the building including the church building was started. Educated members for fear of witchcraft joined the Free Masonry and AMORC and some had black substances, *ekim*, incised into their bodies. These were done side by side with church membership. David Onwuchekwa notes "Western Civilization, might have brought with it religious worships of varied nature but the people of Nnewi, the technological heartbeat of Igbo land are yet attached to the age-old traditional ways of life some of which they believe are responsible for the successes they record in a business venture." So also, were the people of Adadia Circuit and beyond, glued to their fathers' mode of worship.[33]

Above notwithstanding, the mission had created awareness among the people. A vacuum that needed to be filled had been created that only Christ and His message could fill. With this background the events following were a natural consequence, perhaps to make them know the God they did not fully understand.

The Emissary from Adadia: The Primitive Methodist Mission Option

The arrival of Birch Freeman on 24th September 1842 in Badagry marked the effective beginning of Missionary enterprise in Nigeria. Ajayi remarked that "The Rev. Thomas Birch Freeman, energetic Superintendent of Methodist

Mission at Cape Coast, who has shown outstanding abilities by his accounts of his two visits to Ashanti, was asked to occupy Badagry as an outstation of Cape Coast."[34] This he did by capturing Southwestern Nigeria for the Methodist Mission while the Southeastern side of Nigeria was left unattended to. Fortunately, Reverends Fairley and Ben Showell of the Primitive Methodist Mission were at hand to explore Southeastern Nigeria. The Primitive Methodist Mission, notes Essien, "came to Southeastern Nigeria in 1893 and it established a station at Archibong and James Towns. Their work started to flourish as they won new converts".[35]

Soon after they reached Oron, despite the termination of the work of the Church of Scotland Mission in Adadia in 1906, the people had been left with sufficient enthusiasm for Christ and the church. It was to fill the vacuum that Essien Itam, one of the teachers of the defunct Church of Scotland Mission informed Adadia people of the existence of the Primitive Methodist Mission in Oron. Obong Bassey Ekpo, recalls that "Obong Ekanem Ekpo Uta again financed the second search for another Christian religion. This was a Macedonian call to the Primitive Methodist Mission to come to Adadia. The team according to Obong Bassey Ekpo included Effiong Etim, Effiong Inyang Udo, Edet Eduok,

John Udo Orok, Inyang Asuquo Adiaha Umo, Obot Akpan Nnana, Nyong Udo Obot and Offiong Ita. Their charge was simple: to bring the Primitive Methodist Mission to Adadia." They accomplished this task in 1907 when they invited the Primitive Methodist Mission at James Town to Adadia, and that date marks the beginning of the Methodist Church in Adadia.[36]

The missionaries that visited Adadia frequently although not residents, were Reverends N. Boccock; W. Christie and G. H. Hanney. Wards writes that "Christie's health showed signs of giving way."[37] The missionaries were assisted by some Christians of slave origin; like Ekpe Anie Mikue, Mma Deborah, and John Coast Boy. They had tried to base at Ekeya to evangelize the mainland part of present Akwa Ibom State and beyond as their aim was to find a land route to Ikot Ekpene. But as it turned out to be, the climate and lie of the land at Ekeya were not favourable for habitation by the Europeans, but when Rev. Christie wrote, "there is another town of considerable size named Adadia beautifully situated on a high hill 24 miles from Oron", and happening at the time when they were invited by Adadia in 1907 they saw the much-needed opportunity to start the Primitive Methodist Mission in Adadia where the swamp will give way to solid grounds.[38] They did not reside in Adadia.

As itinerant Ministers, they visited Adadia from time to time. All this changed in 1909. Okpo writes "In September 1909, the Rev. F. W. Dodds arrived to take charge of the church at Adadia."[39] Dodds did not go as a resident minister, as his mission was to find a land route to Ikot Ekpene and the heart of Iboe land, Adadia then became a launching pad for the Primitive Methodist Mission to move to other parts of Uruan, Eastern Nigeria and beyond. The Primitive Methodist Mission benefited from the collapse of the Church of Scotland Mission experiment. Rev. Dodds was assisted by Rev. T. W. Hancox and they started the first conscious effort to plant Methodist Mission in Adadia. They started to be residents instead of itinerant ministers.[40]

Okpo tried to trace the movement of the Methodist Missionaries and noted Rev. William Christie, "... he reached Ebughu and Oyubia between 1906 and 1907 and with his pioneering zeal and Christian fortitude pushed into Odobo Okobo, Ekeya and passed to Eastern Nsit and Adadia areas in 1907, after two years Adadia became a circuit".[41] Detailed as the description may be, it tries to dwarf the sacrifices of Adadia people if it is accepted that Methodism first reached Eastern Nsit before Adadia. The truth is what has been stated earlier. Adadia people sent for Methodist Missionaries through the information they got from Essien Itam, following the collapse of the Church of Scotland Mission in 1906. In 1907 the missionaries reached Adadia before spreading to other areas, including Nsit which was evangelized in 1915 when the church reached Ikot Akpabio from Adadia. This also will put Mr M. M. Familusis' idea correct.[42]

Consolidation

In January 1910 Rev. Dodds stepped into Adadia as the first resident Minister. He lived in the house constructed for seventeen pounds at Odoro Nsai This spot is behind late Akpan Ibanga's compound and faces the slope leading to Ibeno Adadia. Both the Manse and the church were built there. In 1911 Rev. E. E. Pritchard came. He caused the church to be removed to Anwa Roberts where Apostolic Church now has her base. The ministers continued to live at Odoro Nsai until later in 1914 when the Ministers demanded a change of environment because of loneliness. There was also the prevalence of wild animals like deer, lion, and leopard, which constituted a threat to lives. Then came the windstorm of that year that removed the roof of the manse. The manse had to be shifted to the site at Etok Ukpa, otherwise called Enwang Iban, or the Old Mission Hill.[43] A Primary School was also built there. As the school grew, it became necessary for a new site to be found. Thus, both the school and the manse were transferred to a new site at Okpoto Nkpok. The school and the Manse are still located at this new site today. When the school left the old site, a zinc roof house was left behind. The church transferred to the small house where the school was because the zinc was better than the mat roof, and remained there till the Jubilee Celebration in 1957 when its inadequacy was exposed. The high turnout from the whole circuit could not be contained in the building. Adadia Church decided then to build a bigger church whose foundation was laid in 1958 by Rev. James E. String-Fellow, B.D.[44]

We may not easily remember all that took place there during the past fifty years. From what we saw and heard, 2 King 22:8 guided the actions of Rev. String-Fellow in laying the foundation stone of the church building. It was felt that when in future the ground was dug and there was none to testify, the bottle that was buried in the foundation would speak. The bottle contained all the names of the members of the church committee at the time. Samples of currency were in use at that time and coins were put in the bottle together with their covenant to serve the Lord with their whole heart. They were sincere and gave them all to prepare for the future. The man who was to impact greatly and permanently on the town and church was Rev. Ernest Pritchard who stayed in Adadia for seventeen years (1911 - 1928).[45]

Figure 1: The Revd. E. Pritchard (1911 - 1928)[46]

Source: Ekpenyong Duke, *100 Years of Methodism in Adadia Circuit 1907-2007, 1992,*p.12

He arrived in January 1911. The Jubilee publication notes of Rev. Pritchard, "Rev. Dodds moved to Bende in January 1911 and in April 1911 Rev. Ernest E. Pritchard came to Adadia, his wife joining him in 1913, to give an invaluable 17 years of concentrated service thoroughly establishing the new circuit". At the time he arrived, the churches were at Adadia in 1907, Issiet Ekim in 1909, Ikot Otoinye in 1910 and Nna Enin in 1911. There appeared a lull in evangelism until 1914 when tragedy struck, and the roof of their house was blown off. He then packed into the pan-roof church while using the Government Rest House for services. Work then started to spread as they lived near the people who interacted with them freely. Rev. Pritchard himself confessed in the publication, "Now they scarcely ever left us. It was the beginning also of the mass movement which affected all our mission stations. By 1918 we had 36 places." The work he did include a class meeting that he held on his verandah for women, the wife helped him with the work. They taught the people reading, writing, sewing, singing, and home keeping. In 1916, Muriel, his wife, established the Junior Christian Endeavour group which aided in teaching women religion and morality.

The Spread

Having been satisfied that his work of consolidation in Adadia was completed, Rev. Ernest Pritchard then started to venture out. He had no bicycle nor a car like today's ministers. His only means of transportation was to trek or to be pulled in a cart or carried in a net. He would sit on the cart and Adadia people would pull him to his next destination in a kind of relay. Sometimes, the receiving station would provide the next pullers. This was how Rev. Pritchard was carried from place to place in the hand cart with two wheels which is still there at Adadia

and produced here to testify to what Adadia people passed through to establish

Methodism in the circuit and beyond. He was sometimes carried in a net-like bag

like a kangaroo would do to its babe.

Figure 2: Rev. Amba, Adadia Circuit Priest in a cart

Source: Ekpenyong Duke, *100 Years of Methodism in Adadia Circuit 1907-2007, 1992,*p.13

With the cart and the net, the Bible was taken from Adadia to Issiet Ekim

in 1909 to replace the Church of Scotland Mission. Ikot Otoinve had their turn in

1910 while Nna Enin had it in 1911. Both Ituk Mbang and Ikot Esse/Ndon Uruan

embraced Methodism in 1914. Ekpene Ibia had its turn in 1912 and all the

churches were grouped into the Uruan. In Etoi Group Rev. Pritchard entered Obot

Obom in 1912. In 1913 Methodism moved to Ifa Ikot Okpon and Mbak Akpan

Ekpenyong and Ifa Atai had a touch of Methodism in 1914, and they formed the Etoi Group.

Another group of churches was the Ibesikpo Asutan Group. The first to embrace Methodism was Ikot Akpa Etok in 1911, Edem Ibiok in 1912 and Ikot Nkim in 1914. He then spread to the Nsit group to establish churches at Ikot Akpabio in 1915, Idiaba in 1917, Ikot Inyang 1919, and Odot 1919 and both Ikot Eket and Ikot Abiyan became Methodists in 1927 in Nsit Group. Rev. Ernest Pritchard prosecuted his job like a bulldozer. He was in preaching as he was in administration. He was in healing as he was in Education. His pioneering work accounts for why he will never be forgotten in Adadia. His social life stands him out as a role model. He stopped the mothers. A typical case was at Nna Enin. A mother of twins had been deprived of her children, who were abandoned in the forest to be eaten by wild animals and ants. This is well illustrated in the wise saying of the people that the day someone finds fortune he does not spend much time looking for it. The story goes thus, the vulture used to fly to the forest, for several days without finding food. In anger, the vulture promised not to call to the forest again. The forest begged the vulture as he was passing and returning to call, for on its lucky day he may not know, or look down.[51]

Fig 3: Mrs Muriel Pritchard and Affiong Nna Enin

Source: Ekpenyong Duke, *100 Years of Methodism in Adadia Circuit 1907-2007, 1992,***p.15**

One day, the vulture called when dead bodies had been deposited for decomposition. The vulture made a meal of them, and the forest reminded him that it had asked him to call always for he may not know his lucky days. That proverb was coined to illustrate that the forest was always rich in dead bodies of smallpox victims and bodies of abandoned twins. Rev. Pritchard met such a scene at Nna Enin. One of the twins had been eaten up by ants and a vulture. He rescued the second one and named her Afiong Nna Enin after the name of her village. He made the girl a Mission child. Eight kilometres from Adadia was covered on foot through a thick forest, infested with wild animals and barbaric customs. He defeated not only the cruel customs but also the wild animals and fearful snakes.

It is to the credit of the missionaries that today, twins are admired and desired and not thrown away or killed.[53]

Fig 4: Little Mission Girls

Source: Ekpenyong Duke, *100 Years of Methodism in Adadia Circuit 1907-2007, 1992*,p.12

The church brought activities of heathen worship under control although not without a fight. In Ifa Ikot Okpon blood was shed and the same was true of Ikot Akpa Etok. Yet Jesus and His Blood took control. Wherever they went, there was a mass movement towards Christianity. The Blood of Jesus had taken violent hold on many towns and villages thereby sending scores of shrines in flames. Pritchard personally recruited Bassey Ekpo, Edet Nsikak and Etim Edet Udo of blessed memories to live with him as servants. All these his servants grew up to be responsible men in government service. He took Daniel Okon Ekpo Bassey to England and trained him as a minister. Bassey Ekpo was later to challenge the Nkanda Ekpe to play with a bottle of water when the players disturbed the church procession. It was no mean feat in those days. The design and plans of churches and houses were what Pritchard undertook to do. He built churches, schools, bookshops, dispensaries, staff quarters and worship centres. He was an experienced photographer and with his knowledge, he kept alive the events of 1907 to 2007, and beyond. As a linguist, he interacted with the people and translated the Gospel and hymns into the Efik language. He classified and wrote the official grammar of the Efik language. As a judge, he awarded justice to villages and the people.[55]

Fig 5: Obong Bassey Ekpo (Pritchard's Mission Boy)

Source: Ekpenyong Duke, *100 Years of Methodism in Adadia Circuit 1907-2007, 1992*,p.17

In 1917 he and Rev. N. Boocook represented the Methodist church in the Aba Conference which discussed the denominational boundaries of churches and the Qua Iboe Church in particular. At the end of the discussion, a church union was set up by the colonial masters whereby once a church had been established in a particular place other churches were to keep off the area. Schools were sited side by side with the churches. The schools provided the light while the churches prepared the heart to accept the light. It is to his credit that before he left Adadia in 1928 he had sowed the mustard seed that was to grow into an enduring tree for if a man's life should be measured in terms of his achievements, his joys, his sorrows, his aspirations and above all his contribution to the happiness of his fellowmen, then surely Rev. Ernest Pritchard was a man, for he had tasted all of these.[57]

Before Rev. Ernest Pritchard left Adadia in 1928 to be succeeded by Rev. A. J. Hawkins, he had divided Adadia Circuit into five groups of Uruan, Ibesikpo Asutan, Etoi, Okobo and Nsit. These groups were later to grow to attain circuit status. Iman Ikono Ibom was later added. For the Uruan group, there was Adadia

1907, Issiet Ekim 1909, Ikot Otoinyie 1910, Nna Enin 1911, Ekpene Ibia 1912, Ituk Mbang, Ikot Ese/Ndon Uruan 1914 and Ibiaku Issiet 1931, Ikot Akpa Ekang 1984 and Nung Ikono Ufok 1986. In 1991 a preaching post was established in Esuk Odu. For Ibesikpo Asutan, the following churches were established: Ikot Akpa Etok 1911, Ikot Nkim 1914, Oku 1915, and Ikot Essien 1952. Ikot Obio Ata 1961, Mbierebe Akpawat 1963, Afaha Udo Eyop 1963 and Ikot Ide Etukudo 1990. Etoi group comprised Obot Obom 1912, Ifa Ikot Okpon 1913, Ifa Atai 1914, Mbak Etoi 1914, Anyanya 1914, Ikot Essien, Itiam, Afaha Ibesikpo, Oku, Ekit Itam, Uyo 1960, Obio Etoi 1961, Use Offot 1975 and Utit Uruan.[58]

Nsit Group comprised Ikot Akpabio 1915, Idiaba 1917, Odot 1919, Ikot Enua 1919, Ikot Abiyan 1927, Ikot Akpan Abia 1952, Ntit Oton 1958, Ikot Adak Okop 1958, Ikot Akpan Ike, Ikot Ubok Udom, Ikot Eket, Ubetim, Ikot Akpabin, Ikot Abasi, Ikot Eyo, Ikot Otu, Ikot Ekpot, Ikot Inyang, Ikot Ebita, Ikot Nkpene, Ikot Ekong, Ikot Edebe, Afaha Nsit, Ikot Essien, Ndukpo Ise, Ikot Ekwere, Ikot Itie Urung with Headquarters at Odot. The earliest Methodist establishment in Nsit was in 1915. So, it was not the first to embrace Methodism. Okobo group consisted of Esuk Inwang 1907. Ebighe Edu, Ebighi Eta, and Ekeya. These Okobo groups of churches were handed over to the Oron circuit for administrative convenience. Iman Ikono Ibom comprised Ikot Ibok Ikot Nte/Obio Eka, Mboito II, Asuna, and Edem Idim Ishiet, all founded in 1957. Both Ikot Nsung Ikono and Efa were added a year later in 1958.[59]

CHAPTER FOUR: IMPACT OF THE METHODIST CHURCH IN ADADIA CIRCUIT

Education

The Planting of churches went side by side with the establishment of schools because the church realized that it would be easier to spread the Gospel to the literate population than to the illiterates. The church of Scotland Mission had started school in Adadia in 1902.[1] The Missionary records in 1903 note "At Adadia town forty children were found but since the number has increased to eighty children regularly attending school."[2] The coming of Rev. Pritchard also aided in the spread of schools. The curriculum of the school included reading, writing, religious knowledge, arithmetic, hygiene, sanitation and singing. Their teachers who were trained at Duke Town School, Calabar included Essien Itam and Edet Abasi Ekpriowo. This school collapsed in 1906 with the Church of Scotland Mission but was revived when the Primitive Methodist Mission took over in 1907. By 1911 the school had spread to other areas and the teaching population had included Joshua Ekpo, George Akpan and Efiom Itor.[3]

The schools turned out disciplined teachers and pupils, who competed in songs, playlets and choral speeches during rallies. The Mission charged fees in their schools. Where school enrolment was low, parents had to pay for empty seats called Assumed Local Contribution or such schools were closed. Fifteen of such schools remain today but were taken over by Government. They are Methodist School - Adadia was founded in 1907, Issiet Ekim in 1909, Obot Obom in 1912, Methodist School Ikot Akpabio in 1915, and Methodist Central School Etoi in 1933. Rev. N. J. Green established Methodist School Odot in 1934 and Methodist School Ikot Ubok Udom in 1937.[4] In 1938 Methodist School Itiam Etoi was founded. Rev. F. W. Bliss opened Methodist School Edebe Akpan Enua now Methodist School, Ikot Akpan Ike in 1947. Methodist School Otu Abiyan was established in 1948 while 1949 saw the emergence of Methodist School Ikot Nkim. Methodist School Ikot Akpa Etok started in 1951, Edem Ibiok, Ikot Otonyie, Ituk Mbang and Methodist School Ikot Ubok Udom, soon sprung up.[5]

To train the increasing number of untrained teachers an Elementary Teacher Training Centre (ETC) was established in Ibiaku Issiet in 1957 by Rev. String-fellow. The teachers followed a Code of Conduct prescribed in the Methodist Standing Orders. Efforts were made to educate the elderly in their

Adult Literacy Centres. Classes were organized in churches where the adults were taught to read and write. These efforts were supplemented by the establishment of the Women Training Centre at Ituk Mbang by Mrs Robbers and Mma Love. Higher Education suffered neglect as none was established in Adadia from 1907 to date. The E. T. C. at Ibiaku Issiet was closed in 1964, Faithful Methodist sons of Adadia Circuit like Sir E. O. Onyong, Elder Okon Edet Essien, Sir E. Duke, Mr E. A. U. Nsikak, and Chief Akpabio Inyang worked hard to establish a secondary school to replace the E. T. C. in 1973 after eight years of neglect. Elder Okon Edet Essien deserves a special mention for his contribution as Group Steward, the leader in the circuit and a pillar of strength for the current Akwa Uruan Circuit.[6]

School Management was excellent. General Manager stayed at Ikot Ekpene to be assisted by a supervisor of schools based in Oron and a visiting teacher was appointed to inspect schools for standards. Mr D. U. Ntuk was based at Ituk Mbang and was the first visiting teacher. The first General Manager was Mr W. T. Smith to be followed by Mr S. K. Okpo who was replaced by Mr E. E. Nsa. These men were assisted by Mr G. N. Igwe and Mr E. N. Ekpo as Supervisors of schools. Man-power development suffered neglect before and after the 1957 Jubilee Celebration. The home Mission did not consider it expedient to train indigenes in higher institutions. A few African servants were sent to the Primary school. Pritchard notes, of the first four boys taken into our homes eleven years ago, one was hopeless, but another is at present on the teaching staff, one is this year finishing the course at Oron Institute and the least is with us in England for special training.[7] The one taken to England was bong Daniel Okon Ekpo Bassey for training in Theology.

Unfortunately, racial segregation played a trick on him as the English Ministers objected to his being trained in an institution that also trained the whites. The dislike followed him to the college and back. He completed his course and passed. He returned to Adadia in 1925. His certificate was never released to him. He was instead of the church, attached to Mma Robberts to work in the Dispensary. To make ends meet he started playing Brass Band for primary school pupils as a hobby. By the time his certificate was released to him in the late 1940s, it had been defaced by termites and thus ended his suffering at Birmingham University. He set up a small business to train his children from the proceeds. When he died in 1986, he had the satisfaction that he had served his God. Atim Etim Effiong was taken by Rev. String-fellow to England in 1960 to train as a nurse. Hers were successful.[8] The government punctuated the Missions management of the school in 1969 when it took over management of schools from voluntary agencies. What the church does now is to extend pastoral care to her schools. She also takes interest in secondary school Adadia, Comprehensive Secondary School, Ikot Akpa Etok and Comprehensive Secondary School Ikot Essien. Preaching appointments are also held at Comprehensive Secondary School Asutan Ekpe. In the primary school section, Government allows the schools to bear their voluntary agency names while the government takes care of management. There is an effort to persuade the government to hand over the schools' management to the church.[9]

Women's Development

As earlier stated, women's work started at Pritchard's verandah led by his wife. Miss Love, Shepherd and Roberts came in later to expand the work to Ituk Mbang. They trained women and girls in mother craft with lectures on cookery, laundry and childcare, child delivery, sewing and home management. Their work was greatly enhanced by the arrival and services of Missess Brazier, Gaderner, Marga Clerk and Ellen Wragg. African women such as Ikwo Edet Itor, Nkoyo Bassey Udo, Ikwo Ekpenyong Duke, Nkoyo Edet Inyang, Nkoyo Okon Nnsemo,

Akon Archibong, Arit Thomas, Arit Peter, Ant Otu, Nkoyo Eka and a host of others were at hand to move women's work ahead. Ikwo Edet Itor notes "They taught us during retreat how to pray and read the Bible in the early hours of the morning, thereafter, followed lectures on child delivery, sewing, needlework, cookery, laundry and childcare".[10]

They formed the women into a committee of 16 made up of four women per group of Uruan, Etoi, Nsit and Ibesikpo Asutan. They used badges to distinguish them from non-members. Women rotated appointments from group to group but were based on merit. What women do now engage in rallies and raise funds for the church? They visit the poor and give them assistance. At the time Adadia was a one-church circuit the women were led by Mrs Nkoyo Ita Udoh, and she gave the women purposeful leadership without which Adadia could not have survived the crises. Elder Mrs Rose Ekaeba succeeded her. Currently, the women are led by Elder (Mrs) Nkoyo Ita Eduok. Responsible women assist her such as Lady Basset' Duke, Elder Mrs Iquo A. Nyong, Elder Ikwo Essesien Eda, Elder Ikwo E. A. Bassey and Many others. Mrs Amba, the wife of the Priest gives them spiritual leadership. They buy chairs, plates and canopies and put them on hire to raise funds.[11]

Health

The health sector received great attention from the missionaries. From the lowly beginning at the verandah of Rev. Ernest Pritchard in 1911 at Adadia health care received a great boom. Pritchard opened a dispensary in his verandah for tablets and sore treatment in a building with three rooms, for a dispensary, carpentry, and bookshop. Quality exercise books were sold in the bookshop. When it started there were in the words of Ernest Pritchard, "small cut to dress and one bottle of stomach mixture to dispense."[11] This soon changed as people flocked to them for treatment. Rev. A. H. Richardson had a love for medical services and took care of the patients. The work was so much that he limited treatment to three times a week, to allow for evangelism.

In 1922, Rev. E. E. Pritchard remarked "These increasing demands were finally met to our great joy by two nurses being sent to us. Miss Roberts and Miss Shepherd did wonderful and sacrificial work. The latter was an expert in Midwifery - but she had to do two heartbreaking tours before she was called to a normal one."' They spent a few months at Adadia while their house was being built. They were first stationed at Ifa Ikot Okpon because the hospital had been moved to Ifa Ikot Okpon in 1929 because of the desire of the missionaries to find a land route to Ikot Ekpene and beyond. Dr Scott, a medical Doctor, was later sent to them and decided to keep his headquarters there. Dr Morris later joined them to share in the spade work. From Ifa Ikot Okpon it was transferred to Ituk Mbang in 1931 because of the presence at Ituk Mbang of perennial water supply, which Ifa Ikot Okpon lacked.[12]

Secondly, a motorable road was constructed through Ituk Mbang to link Uyo with Oron. Ituk Mbang was nearer to Adadia for easy consultation than Ifa Ikot Okpon and so reduced the travelling cost of Miss Roberts and Miss Shepherd, and later Miss Love. It must be noted that of all the Methodist stations along Uyo/Oron Road, only Ituk Mbang is blessed with all-season spring water which is very vital to medical work. These reasons put to rest the assumption of Okpo Edet that the hospital was transferred to Ituk Mbang from Ifa Ikot Okpon because according to him "the work of Ifa Ikot Okpon was interrupted badly. Many of the parents withdrew their daughters and gave them for marriage. This, to them, was more profitable. However, that was the standard of that age".[13] In sum, the hospital moved from Adadia to Ifa Ikot Okpon to allow full-time religious work; from Ifa Ikot Okpon to Ituk Mbang to get fresh water and be near

Adadia and lastly to enjoy the new main road from Oron through Ituk Mbang to Uyo and Ikot Ekpene.

The reason for the transfer must be found in points earlier raised than in marriage intervention. This then justified what Brian Holmes noted when he said "No longer must medical work be regarded as an adjunct to preaching or as a philanthropic agency. It must be a means of education." The missionary preached, healed, and taught. Their subjects included reading, writing and simple Home Economics. A clinic where pregnant women and children were trained and cared for was established. In 1922, Dr Miller joined the healing crew to be followed by Dr Maurice in 1933. But by far the man who left an enduring legacy was Dr Harry Haigh. When he arrived in 1935, he raised the standard of the hospital to an enviable height. He had patients from far away Enugu, Lagos and Nsukka. With the rapid growth in clinical activity and the urgent need for trained nurses, Dr Haigh established a training school for nurses and midwives, the first school of nursing outside Lagos and in this part of the country. The school was patronized by the government, native authorities, and private and other voluntary agencies.[14] Graduates of Dr Haigh's school included Joe Etim Esifa, Inyang Nuwak, Udo Udo Ekwere, Okon Udo Afia, Asuquo Mbaba Ottu, Lucy G. Ubeng, Bassey Efiong

Akpan, Bassey Umo Ekanem and Eno Bassey Mfon to mention but a few. Special mention must be made of the missionaries' effort to improve African lives. A Methodist maternity village was opened at Ituk Mbang. Pregnant women left their homes to live in the maternity village at about seven months of pregnancy. There, they were taught how to care for their expected babies, how to care for themselves, trained in physical exercise and care of the home and were taught some sewing in preparation for the expected baby.[15]

The Social Impact

The impact on the social scene is true of epochal significance. The missionaries were the "pathfinders of the British influence" and certainly assisted the British to consolidate the conquest, especially through the mission schools and missionary influence on the people. The carpenters, masons and bricklayers, trained in the Christian workshops, helped to diffuse the art of their trade in the Region. New forms of house furniture were popularized. The frock replaced the semi-nudity of the women. The lion cloth was exchanged for pairs of shorts, sometimes complete with stockings and shoes. New culinary habits of food and beverages as well as new mannerisms and etiquette became symbols of social prestige. It was easy to pick out a convert in the crowd by his personal attire or social manners. Eating with a fork and knife, seated at the dining table replaced the earlier squatting on the floor and the licking of the fingers. The blessings of literacy, new standards of sanitation and modern scientific medicine were objects of wonder and curiosity. The Christian contribution to the creation of the new social order was, indeed, significant. Some of the earliest mission schools in Adadia.[16]

The Religious Impact

It is the religious sphere that the Christian missions in Adadia left their most telling imprint on the indigenes. In 1846, there were hardly any Christians in the region. By 2008, the objective of founding Christianity in Adadia remains, hope for the future because the foundation has been substantially laid. The religious impact is greatest in three areas of church life: doctrine, ritual, and administration. The rich heritage of religious symbols familiar to the converts was rejected. The Bible is translated into the people's language for proper and better understanding, while the training in Christian morality became casuistic and legalistic. Many denominations have seminary institutions for the training of Church workers.[17]

Political Impact

Sunday Mbang served the Methodist Church as its prelate and National Chairman of the Christian Association of Nigeria (CAN). Many elites of the area are products of mission schools. Educated elites have excelled in local, national, and international spheres of their endeavours. Thanks to Western education. The earliest Akwa Ibom nationalists were products of missionary institutions and exposure. The influence of local, missionaries and resources (catechist-teacher, members of the village Church committees, the generality of the converts and school children) are vital to the success of Christianity in the area.

CHAPTER FIVE: SUMMARY AND CONCLUSION

Summary

The study examined the history of Methodist Church Adadia in the Uruan Local Government Area, 1907-2010. From the study, after the Niger Expedition, the Methodists were the first to exert Christian influence on Nigeria doing so with the arrival of William de Graft and Thomas Birch Freeman in Badagry on 23 September 1842. The story of the arrival of protestant missionaries in Nigeria came as a result of a strong plea that came from a returnee like James Ferguson and this plea was endorsed by the Governor of Badagry. The Primitive Methodist entered Eastern Nigeria with the arrival of Robber Farley in December 1893 from Fernando Po. Both merged in 1932 to form the Methodist Missionary Society. The study shows that Adadia town is located about sixteen kilometres East of Uyo, Akwa Ibom State Capital. It is the terminus of the land route from Uyo through Ifa Ikot Okpon and Mbak Etoi to Adadia. Another route into Adadia is Ibiaku Issiet or Ituk Mbang. The two villages are located on Uyo/Oron Road. The last route is through the sea. This sea route is strategic to Adadia. The Creek meanders into the Calabar River and the Atlantic Ocean. They pointed out that the arrival of Birch Freeman on 24th September 1842 in Badagry marked the effective beginning of Missionary enterprise in Nigeria. The Rev. Thomas Birch Freeman, energetic Superintendent of the Methodist Mission at Cape Coast, who has shown outstanding abilities by his accounts of his two visits to Ashanti, was asked to occupy Badagry as an outstation of Cape Coast. This he did by capturing Southwestern Nigeria for the Methodist Mission while the Southeastern side of Nigeria was left unattended to. Fortunately, Reverends Fairley and Ben Showell of the Primitive Methodist Mission were at hand to explore Southeastern Nigeria.

Soon after they reached Oron, despite the termination of the work of the Church of Scotland Mission in Adadia in 1906, the people had been left with sufficient enthusiasm for Christ and the church. It was to fill the vacuum that Essien Itam, one of the teachers of the defunct Church of Scotland Mission informed Adadia people of the existence of the Primitive Methodist Mission in Oron. Obong Bassey Ekpo, recalls that "Obong Ekanem Ekpo Uta again financed the second search for another Christian religion. This was a Macedonian call to the Primitive Methodist Mission to come to Adadia. The team according to Obong Bassey Ekpo included Effiong Etim, Effiong Inyang Udo, Edet Eduok, John Udo Orok, Inyang Asuquo Adiaha Umo, Obot Akpan Nnana, Nyong Udo

Obot and Offiong Ita. Their charge was simple: to bring the Primitive Methodist Mission to Adadia. They accomplished this task in 1907 when they invited the Primitive Methodist Mission at James Town to Adadia, and that date marks the beginning of the Methodist Church in Adadia.

The missionaries that visited Adadia frequently although not residents, were Reverends N. Boccock; W. Christie and G. H. Hanney. The missionaries were assisted by some Christians of slave origin; like Ekpe Anie Mikue, Mma Deborah, and John Coast Boy. They had tried to base at Ekeya to evangelize the mainland part of present Akwa Ibom State and beyond as their aim was to find a land route to Ikot Ekpene.

Conclusion

From the foregoing, the study of the history of the Methodist Church in Adadia in Uruan Local Government Area has shown to be of immense benefit to the people of Adadia and Uruan Local Government Area as a whole. The history of the Methodist Church in the area has shown that Methodist Church Adadia has been at the forefront of spiritual and social transformation, by spreading spiritual holiness and investing in medical-health services and the socio-economic welfare of the people. The church has established various institutions and carter of the people in the Adadia community. These centres reach out to the rejected and less privileged members of society. They also ensure the reintegration of those previously treated as an outcast and subjected to various societal waves of abuse. In the area of health, Methodist Church Adadia has been known to be providing medical assistance to those with health issues in the community. In addition to all other services, Methodist Church Adadia has from the beginning placed a very strong emphasis on the need for education. Throughout the Adadia community, the church has established schools, from kindergarten through primary to senior secondary school which have produced men and women who have contributed and are still contributing very significantly to all spheres of human endeavour.

Secondary Sources

Ajayi, F. *Christian Mission in Nigeria, 1841-1891,* Hongkong Commonwealth Printing Press Ltd, 1981.

Kanu Austin. *The Role of the Church in Education in Nigeria and the Fundamental Human Rights,* Enugu: Snapp Press Limited, 2008.

Ukpong, David. *Ikono, the Cradle of Ibibio Nation,* Uyo: Dornad Publishers

Duke, E. *Chieftaincy Institution in Adadia Town of Uyo Division,* University of Nigeria, Nsukka, 1997.

Duke E. *Adadia Circuit: Today and Yesterday,* Government Printing Press, Uyo, 1992.

Ekong, Ekong. *Sociology of the Ibibio*, Calabar: Scholars Press, 1983.

Essien, Dominic. *Uruan People in Nigerian History,* Modern Business Press, Uyo,1993.

Kalu, O. *The History of Christianity in West African Essays Lectures*, London:

Longmans Groups, 1980.

Nwaka, Calabar: "A Colonial Casualty - Calabar: Cross River State Newspaper Corporation, 1976" *The Calabar Historical Journal* Vol.1 No.1, 1976.

Noah, M. *Ibibio Pioneer in Nigerian History,* Calabar, Cross River State News Paper Corporation, 1980.

Okon, Edet Uya, *The History of Oron people of the Lower Cross River Basin,* Oron: Mason Publishers Co.

Oshitelu, *Expansion of Christianity in West Africa*, Abeokuta: Visual Resources Publishers, 2002.

Okpon, Otobong E. *The History of Akwa Ibom State and Her 31 Local Government Areas at a Glance,* Uyo: Robertou Communications Publishers

Parrinder, *Africa's Three Religions*, London: Sheldon Press, 1969.

Udo, Ema. *Ekpe Society*. Nigerian Magzine, 1938, Vol.16.

Uruan Local Government Area | IbomYellowPages. www.ibomyellowpages.com. Retrieved 2023-02-26.

Wards, *In and Around the Oron Country*, London: Longmans Groups Ltd, 1980.

Unpublished Works

Koko Ina, " *The Okuku Ibiono Ibom from Origin to Present*", M.Phil. Thesis, Department of History, University of Calabar.

Ekaette Akra, "*The Pre-colonial Agricultural History of Ibiono Ibom*", A B.A Research Project, Department of History, University of Calabar, 1979.